I0165129

CONVERSATIONS WITH
A
WHITE WALL

C.E. Nelson

RADIANT SKY
PUBLISHING GROUP

Copyright © 2016 Chad Nelson
Radiant Sky Publishing Group

All rights reserved.
Edited by Amanda Terry
Contributions to the poem "Cool Kids"
provided by Aisha Razzak

ISBN-13: 978-0692727133
ISBN-10: 0692727132

to Kim,

I promised.
Here you go, fucker.

Section I

Sometimes, when you scream into the void, it does nothing

Sometimes, it echoes

What on earth are you rambling about now?

Is this going to be some more of your existential bullshit?

No, it's the first section of my book.

Read 2:49 PM

THE RORSCHACH TEST

I don't know how to
explain my mind to
someone else.

Some children are scared of
lightning storms.

Now, just imagine,
you are both
the lightning and
the child.

GOD CAN'T DO LAUNDRY

God?

I prayed to you once,
but you didn't answer.
I've got this disease.
This disease
that everyone has
but no one knows the cure.
It's called
loneliness.

I drown my pain
in liquid detergent.

They tell me
that bleach gets the blood out,
but I ain't had my
prayers answered yet.

BUT JESUS CAN

I am at church,
somewhere I haven't been
since I was a child.
I sit and listen to the
sermon.
It is about Jesus.
It's always about
Jesus.

The priest is reading a passage.
I think about lunch.
They will be serving
a piece of bread
in a moment, and that will
quell my hunger for
the time being.

They start to sing a hymn
as the people begin to go up
for Communion.

I wait my turn and walk to the priest.

He breaks bread.

Someone breaks wind.

They both stink
but I take the crumbs
knowing Heaven is
vacant.

BEARDS & FLANNEL

Oh, you, full of such
sensitivity,
such kindness,
such tenderness,
such silly traits.
These are not the features of a
MANLY
man.
No, a
MANLY
man drinks the whiskey
because it puts the hair
on his chest and the sperm
in his balls, and a
MANLY man fucks the women
with his big ol' thunderous
cock
because all the women must know how
big
and
thunderous
his cock is so he can justify
being a
MANLY
man.

I mean, all women like it when manly
men sneak off in the middle of the night,
right?

Right?

There's More Than One Shade Of White

Some nights,

I lie on my couch and
I stare off into a corner
of my kitchen that sits
adjacent to my living room
and there's a white wall there,
just like there's a white wall
all over this fucking apartment.
But, this particular white wall
is covered by white
kitchen cabinets.

Cream, they're cream color.

No, eggshell.

Navajo white. (I found that in
the thesaurus, but Stephen King
said not to use a thesaurus
because if the word you need
isn't in your head, then it's the
wrong word. Well, fuck you
Stephen, you redruming asshole.)

And, some nights,
when there's too much going on
in the world,
I lie on my couch
and converse with a white wall
and pretend I'm not crazy.

BOILING WATER

You go to eat the
macaroni
because the
macaroni
is all that's in the pantry
and you sift through the
drawers to grab a fork
and you search the fridge
to find the butter
but the forks are dirty
and you can't locate the butter
so you can't make the
macaroni
but you did come across
a bit of

madness

and that will fill you up for tonight.

I SAW A MAN KILL HIMSELF ONCE

Sometimes, the
knife
is cold
and sometimes the
pills
are chalky
but you make a choice
and you
stick with it.

Mac & Cheese

I'm all out of fucking milk
and I have nothing to wash
this mild salsa off my tongue
with, and I'd go grocery shopping
but I'm not terribly good at that.
You see, I was married for 14 years,
and I'm not good with taking
care of myself, and I know
that's not an excuse but this
is the first time in 34 years I've
lived by myself, and I didn't go
to college, and I know that's not
an excuse, but I only know how
to make Mac and Cheese and
I'm all out of fucking milk.

MILENA

You wake up and you're not the person
you thought you were.
You're a little more hardened
and a lot more wrinkled.
There's more silver
than there is black.
You're everything you didn't want to be,
and nothing you should have been.

It's lonely here; a tugboat on a sea of yachts.

I wake up and I'm all the experiences of
everyone else, and none of my own.
I am a re-run of biblical proportions.
Do I really remember my first girlfriend
waving goodbye to me from her second story
window, or was that a TV show?
Did my friends really sling dope in high school,
or was that one of those "next time on a very
special Blossom" episodes?

I remember my hopes in fragments, in pieces.
I am not whole, I haven't done enough.

I wake up and I am not the person
I thought I was.

PREDATORS & PREY

Sometimes the cat goes
crazy.
She chases her tail,
jumps,
bites,
digs her
claws into flesh.
Hisses.
Her eyes get
big and she slouches down
ready to pounce as a feline
predator
and I feed her and give her water
and pet her and give her
attention and affection
but sometimes she just goes
crazy
and I wonder if
humans are all that different.

A REALLY BIG SHOE

There was a gigantic beetle
in my room tonight
and I wasn't quick enough
to crush it before
it ran off behind
the blinds
and now
I am
afraid
it will come to
kill
me.

TINY HEARTS

I gain a pound,
I lose a pound.

Flesh of my flesh,
hound of my hound.

I will weigh less in the morning
than I do tonight.

All of my lovers
scurry off in flight.

Today 2:25 PM

Section II

People leave and then you die

Read 2:26 PM

Well, that's not depressing.

iMessage

Q W E R T Y U I O P

A S D F G H J K L

⇧ Z X C V B N M ⌫

123 ☺ 🎤 space return

Uprooted Trees

They all tell me
of their horrors
and their nightmares
because I can take it.

Because I have eyes
of green forests that
they can hide things in.

I sit there and listen and
smile and
listen and
smile
and I let their pain
break me apart
so that they can stay whole.

But, my well
only runs so deep.
Someone needs to water
my flowers too.

The woods are a terrible
place
to get lost in.

Trees do not hug back.

GONE

I'm giving up.

There's nothing
left here for me these days.
I have nothing to look
forward to anymore.
The days are always the same,
and I can't take the repetition any longer.
I pull myself up from a mattress
on which my feet hang off the edge
because it's too short.
I then walk five steps to the bathroom
and turn on the shower,
and my hardest decision
for the day is
how much I want to burn myself
in the water. I stand there and
wonder how the sum of my life
has added up to nothing.
I then put on a suit meant for a funeral
and head off to a dead end job.

Sometimes, on the way home,
I think about skipping my exit
and just driving. I don't think
there would be much to
disappearing.
I often wonder,
"who would be the first to notice I'm gone?"
and,
"how long would it take?"

I went home recently after some 16 odd years,
and my father almost didn't recognize me
as he walked past.
Maybe I had lost some weight,
maybe I had gained some, I'm not too sure.
All I know,
is that, you don't see a person for awhile
and you forget what they look like.
You don't talk to someone for awhile,
you forget that they even existed.

One day,
I'm going to wake up and
decide to burn myself just a little bit more
in the shower. I'm going to give the cat
a little more food and water than usual.
I'm going to go to my job,
dressed for my funeral,
leave my work keys at the end of the day
and drive past my exit and
disappear.

One day,
you'll wake up and I will be gone.

DISAPPEARED

My lips have started to develop
this numbing,
tingling feeling
as I drift off to sleep.
My whole body has begun to do this,
and I will lie in some stage of
paralysis while my mind wanders.
This must be a sign of getting older.
Maybe it's the
emptiness in me taking over.

She held me once,
and I felt a warmth
radiate from her body.

A light was shining
somewhere,
but it would never
illuminate me.

There is an ocean of
darkness in me,
and the moment I open up to people,
the moment
I let them in,
they drown.

And, I realized,
people don't leave me and
disappear
because they want to.

They disappear because
I kill them.

EMPTY TRAINS ON FAR AWAY TRACKS
DO NOT BLOW THEIR WHISTLE

I remember, decades ago,
when
I sat on the phone.
It was cold in my hand.

The silence seemed to
last eternities.

At last he spoke,
"I'm disappointed in
you, son."

There were train tracks
that ran through the field
behind our house

and the train that went by
that night
made no noise.

It made no fucking noise,
and I remember wondering,
if the dads of the kids
who vandalized the cars
of that train
were
disappointed
in them, or if it was just
my pops.

I wanted him to scream
and yell, or curse at me.

But, he didn't do any of that.
He was calm.

And that train made
no
fucking
noise.

FRACTURES

I've broken many bones
throughout my life.

I broke my wrist
when I was seven. I was practicing
for the high jump portion
of my school triathlon.
The pain was excruciating and
I was in a cast for two months.
It got better quick because
I had my first girlfriend help
me with my homework.

I broke my sternum
from jumping off a swing.
I thought I could fly.
I guess I learned
the hard way that
flying will knock
the wind out of you.
I had trouble
breathing for a week.

I broke a rib
running because I tripped over
my own feet. I told people
that I almost got run over
on my bike and crashed,
because saying that you tripped
over yourself
makes people laugh

and laugh
and call you an idiot.

I broke a finger
playing basketball last week.
It doesn't bend anymore.

But, I think the worst break
I've ever had was when
a rock hit my windshield
the other day
and it was me that cracked
and broke in half.

PUMPKIN GHETTO

They didn't tell me rock bottom
wasn't full of rocks.
Had I known that, I might have
seen this coming, and done my
best to avoid it.

It's empty here.

I've bought stacks and
stacks of books
hoping that reading the lives
of others would somehow
fill mine.
I must have miscalculated.

It's empty here.

I spend most of my evenings
lying on a bumpy mattress and
staring at the ceiling.
I contemplate drawing a bath
and sliding under the water
for a few minutes,
but I'm sure someone
would miss me. Although,
I can count the number of texts
I've received today on one hand
and I don't even need the other hand
to count the number of phone calls I've had.

It's lonely here,

and people have plans that don't involve me.

They didn't tell me rock bottom
wasn't even the bottom.
No, it's actually
a one bedroom, upstairs unit
in the upscale part of the ghetto.
Far away removed from my daughter.
From my friends and family.
Far away from anything
I used to call home.

I decided to take a shower tonight
instead of the bath and
I stood there and picked at
some old scabs and I became
upset that I haven't found
a water temperature hot enough
to wash away pain.

I look to the future and hope
tomorrow
will be better but
tomorrow never comes.
Hope has failed me,
just as people have.
They tell me things, like how much
they care,

but I've read enough fake poets
to know words are empty
unless there is meaning
behind them.

CHEAP DATE

We laugh
and we have a
good time
and for a
moment
I think I'm valuable
and then the
wind
changes direction
and I am
reminded
that I am
nothing special.

Section III

Conversations with a white wall

Really? You're going to use your book title as a section title?

Oh, that's really original.

Read 2:31 PM

Dude, I've already told you I'm more of a cream color.

UNTITLED #1

There is a white wall
in front of me.

I stare at it
until it crumbles.

I tried to love you
until you loved me back.

Mistakes I continue to make.

UNTITLED #2

"Smile, kid.

Don't let them
know you're dying.

They'll try to
kill you faster."

UNTITLED #3

"That's the thing about love,
I suppose.

Some of us can give
it out so easily,

while others
are never ready to accept it."

Untitled #4

"What a travesty.
A god damn travesty
that as children
we are taught that sex is a
disgusting abomination
that should only be
done with the lights off,
while we are told to
champion violence with wide eyes
and wonderment.

Maybe,
if we fucked more
and killed less,
this world would be a better place."

UNTITLED #5

"You know,
I, very much,
dislike
Daylight Savings.

What a ridiculous notion
that we can somehow control
the rise and fall of the sun
by simply changing
the hours
on a pocket watch."

<u>UNTITLED #6</u>

"I am endlessly
sifting through
laundry baskets
for matching socks."

UNTITLED #7

"I try to drown myself in friends
but it is not the same.

They can not give me what I need.

I will never know your touch
from their hands."

Untitled #8

"I don't trust
people anymore.

They'll find a way
to kill you

and then

still make sure
you're
to blame."

UNTITLED #9

"I don't believe in much
but I do believe there is
still good in this world
and it's hiding
behind all of the chaos
we mistake as hate."

Untitled #10

"There are good people out there.
You must seek them out. You'll
find them in the most unlikely
of places, but you'll know them
by how they talk. It's in the way
they say "sorry." Listen to the
pronunciation. You can literally
hear the sincerity in their voice.
Cling to these people. For, somehow,
they have been so wronged in life,
they feel they must apologize for
everything."

UNTITLED #11

"Sometimes,
I sit at work and
wonder what the

fuck

I'm doing
and who my heart's
beating for and
if I have anything to
look forward to
besides death."

UNTITLED #12

"I don't know.
I just feel, ya know,
I feel that you either
give her everything
or nothing at all.

There is no in between
in love."

Section IV

You are larger than a great many things

Love is not one of them

Oh, NOW you're going to be romantic.

I'm always romantic.

Read 2:37 PM

Have you read the first three sections of your book??

MADDI, LET ME CATCH MY BREATH

She wants you to chase her.
So, chase her.

Chase her until your shoes
fall apart, until your feet
have blisters, until your thighs
burn and until your lungs scream.

Chase her until she allows you
to catch up and crash into her
with all of the love you've been
holding for far too long.

Crash into her with such a force so that
she knows you mean it when you
grab hold of her, caressing her
tender skin and kissing her
full lips like they are the only
thing that will give you oxygen.

Then let her go to run off again,
as she gives you a mischievous grin,
a sexy smile and a sly wink.

It's a cycle, boys.
She wants you to chase her.
So, chase her and
don't ever stop.

I'LL DO ANYTHING TO BE YOUR EVERYTHING

Everyone's always
worried
about the
hundred
reasons it won't work

and

I'm sitting here
thinking
of the
one
reason why it will.

THE WORLD AT OUR FEET

She was just
sitting there
on the
passenger side
of the car,
smoking a
cig
and staring out of
the window
with her feet up on
the dashboard
and
every so often
I'd steal
a glance
her way
and remember
what
love was.

SUPERMAN DOESN'T WEAR A CAPE

She called me her hero once,
but I didn't save her
from any fire.
Although, if I were any
other writer,
I'd tell you of how I walked
through the burning gates of
Hell and rescued her from the
clutches of Satan himself.

I didn't take a bullet for her,
although, if I were any
other writer,
I'd tell you of the one time
I played Russian roulette
with her love and lost,

but I'm not,

so, I'll tell you of the time
I made her
smile
and that's how
I saved a life.

WE TALKED ABOUT POETRY ONCE

It started as small talk
as these things often do.

At some point,
I said something
about my
typewriter
and she started to mention
all of my favorite
writers.

When you get to be my
age
you lose all substance of
subtlety.
So, I told her to
come ride my
cock.

Love just ain't what it use to be.

<u>WOMEN</u>

This damn cat
follows me around
my tiny apartment.

All day.
All night.

She curls up
in my lap and
sleeps next to me
in bed.

Finally,

a female who
begs for my
attention.

OB/GYN

She tells me
she loves me
but she also tells
that to the
garbage man when he picks up the
garbage,
and to the gynecologist when he
checks her
hoohah,
so I don't know what to think.

The best I ever did
was write some
lousy
love poems.

CORSETS & BLACK FISHNETS

The women
will drive you crazy,

drive you mad,
drive you to the brink of
insanity

and laugh at you as you
cross the line.

They'll tell you when to
stroke it.
How to stroke it.

They'll kiss you with strawberry lips,
with cocaine
                lips,
with heroin
                lips,
until you become addicted.

Crossing their legs
this way and
that way.
It's hypnotizing.

They wink and they smile
and they slide up and
down,
and it's okay partner,
they know the game better than us,

and they know what makes us hard,
and every now and then
you just lie back and
enjoy the show.

Lustful Animals

She tells me she likes
how loud I get in
the bedroom
and I tell her
that she drives me
crazy
and I still haven't
decided which one of us
is the animal
in all of this.

GREEN BEAN CASSEROLE

Most nights,

the dinner
goes cold
on the counter

and I go
starving

because
the only thing
I've been hungry
for lately
has been

love.

You're A Good Man, Charlie Brown

"You're a good man."
and
"You're a great catch."
and
"You really are quite wonderful."
and
"I appreciate you."
and
"I think the world of you too."

I've heard it all from
women. They usually
forget to leave off the
rest though. The part
that hurts the most.
They forget to tell you
that walking in the middle
of the road is where you
get hit the hardest.

"You're just not good enough for me."

PLEASE REMEMBER, MY HEART IS STILL BEAUTIFUL EVEN WHEN I'M A MONSTER

We yelled at each other
this morning,
so I did the only thing
I could think of to apologize.

I sat at my typewriter and wrote
something for only her to see

and she came over and kissed
my cheek and told me,
"You're a good man, Emery."

"Depends on the day, babe.
Depends on the day." I replied.

I hope she remembers that even
when the green monster in me rages,
it is her voice
that steadies my pulse.

POETRY RULE #2

Writing shitty
love
poems for a
hundred
different women
might get you

laid

but, sooner or
later
brother,
someone is going to
cut
off your

balls.

Section V

And so, I write because my voice cracks

Are you sure it's not puberty?

Fuck you.

Read 2:41 PM

COOL KIDS

I fly over your head.
Do you see me as an Eagle
or the Vulture I really am?

Will you laugh like all the other
school children just to fit in?

Write a haiku; it is both
easy to learn
and harsh to master.

There is a struggle in being brilliant,
ya know.

THE POPSICLES ARE A METAPHOR

I am jealousy.
Steamed broccoli.
I am rage.
Ripened tomatoes.
I am voyeur.
Stalking your windows
and watching you fuck him.
I am remembrance.
Sticky blue Popsicles.
I am lost memories.
Distorted pictures with
cropped heads.
I am late nights.
Wondering when you are
coming home.

LAX To YXE

They bring the drink cart down
the too small aisle of this
too small plane
and she asks me if I want a drink
after she smacks my knee
with the fucking cart

and yes

I want a damn drink
for the throbbing pain
but I ain't had a fucking drink
in six years
because I'm on this
little red pill that's supposed
to cure the disease
but sometimes you just need
something to block out
the dull thud of the world around you.

"Do you have any rum?" I ask.

YXE To LAX

Two and a half
more hours on this plane.

Crack my head open and
I think I might float up here
as long as I can.

I look down, through the
clouds and past the
white tipped mountains and
I see the
tiny people with their
tiny cars and
tiny houses and
tiny pets and
tiny lives.
All of them making terrible
decisions and I think I can

see Heaven from up here

and I think this is as close
to God as I'll ever be.

THERE'S NO MEDALS FOR THIS

I felt myself
catch
cold
yesterday.
So, I drank
a gallon
of
orange juice
straight from the
jug
and I
beat death
because I
am a
winner.

<u>Plagiarism Is Bad Kids</u>

They all really suck.
I mean, they kind of do.
A word
    here
        and a word
      there
and then your name.
Sure, it's writing,
but, it's not exactly
poetry.

Line break.

I ain't never stole before,
except that pack of
gum
in grade school and
I really miss the days
when porn held
my attention.

A Drought In So. Cal

There is a different
type of sun that calls
Southern California home.
It beats down on me until
I catch a fever over my brow;
until I sweat from my
fingernails.

I never did mind that though,
as it gave me the lube to play
the banjo across her thighs.
I killed her,
not once, not twice,
but thrice.

And, mama, aren't you proud of the
man
I've become?

My hand is on fire, and now
I mind. Now, I fucking
mind.
And, I'm blowing it out. I'm blowing
and blowing, and
this fucking sun just keeps beating
down on me, and I perspire from my hair,
and the sun
laughs and smiles
and shines brighter.

Bastard.

ARE YOU SMARTER THAN A SEVEN YEAR OLD?

My daughter asked me what
poetry
was earlier and I did
my best to explain to a
seven year old.

"Poetry can be stories
sometimes, I guess, but usually
it's writing about how you feel."

"Oh, so it's life," she replied

and she obviously knows more than me.

IDEAS AREN'T FORCED

My publisher tells me to write
more.
My editor tells me to write
more.
My friends tell me to write
more.
My girl tells me to write
more.
The mailman tells me to write
more.

"Fuck you, you're the mailman,
what do you know?"

They all think the writing flows
out of me like diarrhea.

I don't shit ideas.
I shit shit.
And by shitting shit, it keeps the shit
in the shitter
and off the page.

It's A Sin To Only Write Quotes

He told me to write for
myself,
so, I did.
Then he read one,
and called it
"Fantastic."

So, I wrote more like
that, but they were
shit,
and now I write
quotes.

HER/SHE

Let her run free during the day,
but make sure to lock her in a cage
at night,
so she knows she's all yours,
and yours alone.
Beat her into submission the next day
with your big ol' cock
and then leave
a love note on the pillow for her
so she knows you are all hers,
and hers alone.

But don't cry for her,
because you're a
man
and you let her run free during the day,
and she needs that.

INADEQUATE

When I was younger,
I worked at a grocery
store and I was so good
at my job, one day, the old man
in charge came up to me and said,
"Hey kid, stop doing so much,
You're making everyone else
look bad."

So, I started to do a real
mediocre job.

A few weeks later he came back up
to me and said,
"Hey kid, you need to
do better."

And, I guess I could never
really make people
happy,
even back then.

SWIMMING WITH THE FISH

Where to begin?
They want me to be happy, or
so they say.
"I'll be happy for you when you
find someone."
But they don't realize that
they make me happy.

Women want a dick with a dick,
not a nice guy with
blue balls.

I called you tonight and you didn't
answer, so I rang her line.

Busy.

I remember our kisses and how I
felt dead inside. Or was that the
hollow in your mouth from your
lies?

There's many fish in the sea, but
I can't count past four.
Next time you call,
I won't pick up.

HOW TO POETRY

She was lightning in a bottle –
ready to strike at any moment.

If you are still reading,
congratulations,
I will now write the same thing from
the first stanza with different words

and this line will tie it all together.

PAINT THINNER

When I was younger
I would help my dad
with home improvements.

Upgrading the bathroom,
fixing cabinets,
new windows, new doors,
painting the walls.

He told me that
paint thinner
was good at cleaning
most messes.

Last week, I went to
the store and bought
four bottles
but, I still haven't
been able to
clean
the
mess
you left behind.

SHE LIKES WHEN YOU SMACK HER ASS

You come home at night
and maybe
you've got a swell family waiting on you
and dinner's ready
and Johnny won his football game
and Amy got an A on her algebra test
and your wife is giving you the
'fuck me' eyes from across the table
and you've got a California King
that you can bend her over
as you smack her ass
and the kids will spend the weekend
with grandma Sue and
life is good and you're
alright
and everything is alright

and maybe

you come home at night
and you walk into an empty apartment
with nothing but a tiny cat waiting on you
and you eat left over
Chinese
and you didn't play football
and you were never good at the maths
and you see your only daughter on the
weekend
and life isn't good
but you hope you'll be
alright

and everything will be alright

and maybe we're all just
dying to be alright.

DEJA VU

It's always the
same.

The same mattress with the bulge
in the middle that I wake up from
every morning.

The same glowing sun that
burns my eyes
every morning.

The same white walls that I hang
loneliness from instead
of pictures.

The same front door with the same
faulty lock that barely keeps
the wolves out at night.

I remember growing up and going
to church where they would tell me,
"Life is glorious."

They forgot to tell me that
glory is spelled
M O N O T O N Y.

CANADIAN WINTERS

I grew up on cold
Canadian
winter streets.
Frozen roads and slick sidewalks.
My lungs would burn
as my breath would sit lazily
in front of my face
and my biggest
challenge
was keeping my nose warm at night.

I miss those days,
when the ice was on the ground
and not in my heart.

VEGAS BABY! VEGAS

I'm on my way up the
Cajon Pass
towards my old home,
and I'm stuck in traffic.
This freeway is the only one
from L.A. to Vegas
and today,
everyone has decided to take a trip
to gamble their soul.

It's hot and I want to stop my car,
get out and go randomly
tap on people's windows and
ask them,
"A penny for your thoughts?"
But, I already know the answer.
They all want to win a
World Series Poker gold bracelet.

'Cause, it's a penny to spin
and a dollar to sin.

They all want to count cards like
Dustin Hoffman
while I memorize phone books.
And, they'll all become
Ray-Ban gods
just because they got comped
rooms and food and shows
and spins and
Blackjack baby!

And now they're all card sharks and
I'm a dolphin.
They may eat me but they'll
never be smarter.
And, even when the house doesn't win –
the house still wins.

'Cause it's a penny to spin
and a dollar to sin.

I Die On These Pages
So I Can Live In Life

You get so exhausted.
You get so
overwhelmed.

Ain't no one coming to

save

you.

You might as well
choke down the pills
and pray you get the chance
to repeat the same
damn thing
tomorrow.

Nobody likes

joyful

poetry.

You best learn that.

Illustration by Paul Rañosa

This is Chad Nelson's second collection of poetry. He still owns a orange couch, and still has an obsession with porn. He now is the proud owner of an annoying cat, but he loves her. His first book is currently available for purchase. He encourages you to read it, but don't compare it to this one.

www.ingramcontent.com/pod-product-compliance
Lightning Source LLC
Chambersburg PA
CBHW020557030426
42337CB00013B/1121

* 9 7 8 0 6 9 2 7 2 7 1 3 3 *